REASON
and
RHYME

JUST FOR JEWISH WOMEN

(And Some Jewish Men)

First published 2013

ISBN 978-1568715759

Comments may be sent to the author at mark6137@aol.com

Published by

Targum Press
PO 27515
Jerusalem 91274

Distributed by

Menucha Publishers INC.
250 44th Street
Brooklyn NY 11232
Tel/Fax: 718-232-0856, Ext 200
1855-Menucha

Printed in Israel

REASON
and
RHYME

JUST FOR JEWISH WOMEN

Dr Mark Gersten

Author's dedication

Dedicated to my wife Helene, *a"h*
My soulmate and partner in life:

I miss her candles Friday night
And faces 'round the table, bright.
Melodies and harmony
Sabbath songs sung gleefully
G-d takes away but also gives
Just look into the life one lives.
My children and their children's traits
Remind me of Helene my mate's
At times I'd look at them, and swear
My darling wife is over there

Acknowledgements

My appreciation and thanks to
The Ribono Shel Olam for giving me
The ability to undertake and complete this book
Dr Gary Chubak for technical support
My family for their understanding
My supporters for their faith in me
And the quality of my work

Introduction

Jewish History provides a rich tradition of role models, both male and female, whom we can learn from and try to emulate. The essence of this poetic work is to identify the Midot (valuable) character traits of the Women of the Bible and Talmud. Although often in the background, they were the inspiration and power source which allowed their husbands and sons shine in the eyes of G-d and man.

Their contributions can never be overstated and should be appreciated by all.

Contents

Your Place

In time, you'll take an honored place
Among the woman of our race
Who found much joy to spend their lives
As righteous women, mothers, wives
Often wiser than the men
With great devotion to Hashem

About Women and Angels

In the morning women pray *'sheasani kirtzono'*
Look to find its meaning and you will come to know
Hashem, your Lord made you, exactly by his plan
With intuition well beyond that of any man.
If angels had their own prayer, it's crystal clear to me
'*sheasani kirtzono*', it would surely be
The angels have no urges and no conflicts like a man
He created them quite differently in his master plan
So much like the angels, are our women, it is true
Their *'neshamas'* close to G-d, their goodness shining through

Women in the Torah

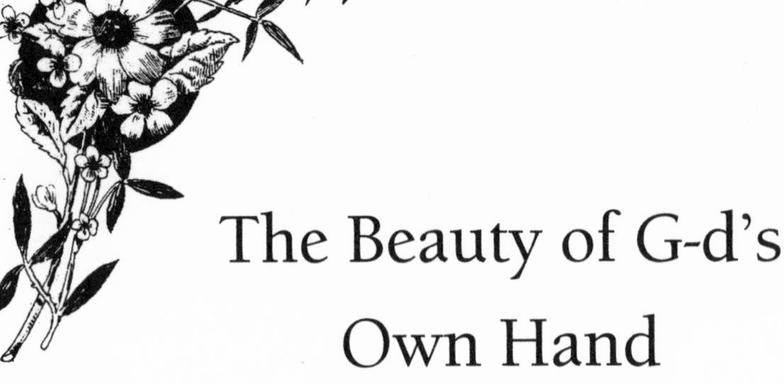

The Beauty of G-d's Own Hand

Eve

No other woman could compare
To Eve's beauty, fine and rare
Created by the Lord's own hand
The mate for Adam that he planned
Bedecked in ornaments of gold
With singing angels we are told
Came to Adam as his wife
Through her came all human life
True, she caused Adam to sin
Or life in Eden would have been
For all mankind and for all time
Spiritual and sublime
But still from her sin we do know
Good from evil, how to grow
Worthy in G-d's eyes and man's
The current purpose life demands

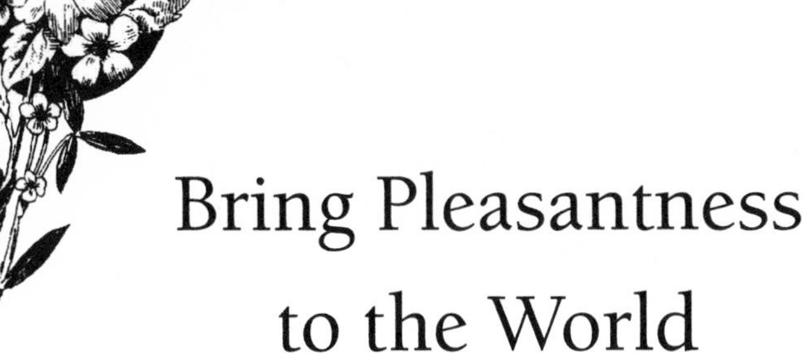

Bring Pleasantness to the World

Naamah

Naamah, Noah's wife, was just as pleasant as her name
Made instruments from iron, but they were not the same
As her brother's sharpened iron implements which kill
Her instruments made music and she played them with great skill
Indeed, Naamah invented both the music with the song
As she played her instruments, she also sang along
She knew things G-d created, were themselves not bad or good
But depend on how they're used, and if used as one should
Naamah used G-d's iron to bring happiness and joy
Her brother Tubal Kayin to bring pain and to destroy

Binah

Sarah

Young Ishmael was a crude, wild lad
When playing with Isaac, Sarah had
Visions of sins that he had done
She felt he would corrupt her son
Abraham torn deep inside
Both sons were his and gave him pride
Sarah understood his pain
Paternal love did still remain
Since Ishmael was from his seed
Though far from him in thought and deed
The future clearly with her son
Who loved and served the Holy One.
"Listen to Sarah, for she does know"
G-d said, "She's right, Ishmael must go,
A greater prophetess than you
Her '*binah*' tells her what to do"

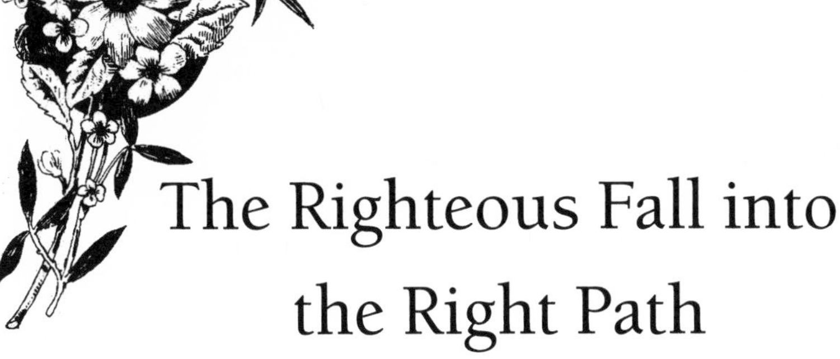

The Righteous Fall into the Right Path

Lot's daughters

His daughters thought G-d did destroy
The whole world, that's the reason why
They tried to save the human race
Through Lot, although they felt disgrace
But sometimes sins conceived for good
Count for merits as they should
We know Moshiach comes through them
The only question left is when

Faithful to a Mate

Hagar

Hagar was a princess and a daughter of Pharaoh
He told her to leave Egypt, it was better that she go
To be a maid to Sarah, the wife of Abraham
A prince of G-d , a prophet, and a truly holy man
In time, she married Abraham and with him had a son
But Ishmael was crude and thoughtless – quite an evil one
Forced to leave the household, Hagar tended to her son
But since she married Abraham, he'd be the only one
Living with this special man no other could compare
A kind man steeped in ethics, of that she was aware
Her other name Keturah, she was like pure incense
After life with Abraham, no other man made sense
Like a dove or turtledove, just one mate in her life
Abraham, once Sarah died, took her back as wife

Carry on Tradition

Rebecca

Rebecca, Isaac's wife was wise
He saw great kindness in her eyes
Yet did not take her to his tent
Until beholding the event:
Her Sabbath candles all week bright
Her *challah* lasted day and night
G-d's cloud remained above her tent
These miracles from G-d were sent
Then Isaac knew she'd take that place
A mother of the Jewish race
With Sarah, Isaac's mother, gone
Rebecca fit, would carry on
As Jewish matriarch and wife
The cherished partner in his life
T'was only then he fell in love
She was his match from G-d above

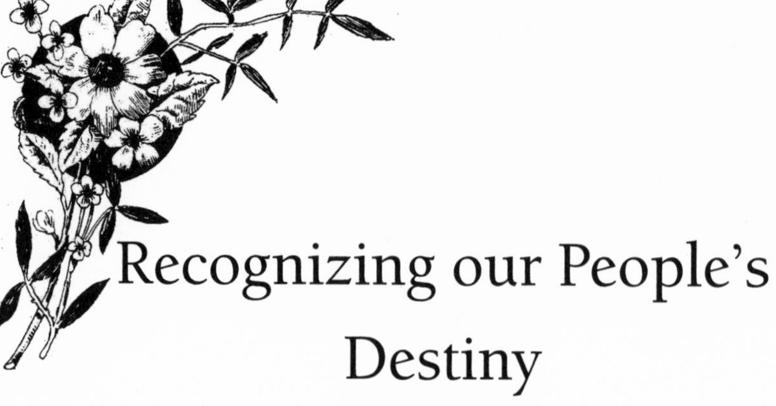

Recognizing our People's Destiny

Rebecca

A host of G-dly angels cried
With Isaac on the alter tied
By Abraham, who heard G-d's voice
Commanding him, he had no choice
The angel's tears fell in both eyes
His vision suffered from their cries
Some say that's why he couldn't see
His son Esau's hypocrisy
Finding truth needs more than eyes
When man pretends and tells his lies
Rebecca, who was Isaac's wife
Knew charlatans throughout her life
Her brother Lavan, the first one
Later came Esau, her son
Isaac thought it Esau's place
To lead those of the Jewish race

But she saw Jacob pure and true
And knew just what she had to do
Make Isaac bless her younger son
For Jacob was the worthy one
For she received a prophesy
Which clearly told her what would be
So she took matters in her hand
And did what she thought G-d's command
Before the blessing made a meal
Which she prepared with careful zeal
Since blessings are best if they start
With peaceful soul and happy heart
Gave Jacob, Esau's clothes to wear
Then hid his smooth arms with goat hair
He fooled his father just that way,
Was blessed as firstborn on that day
Rebecca wise, could clearly see
What Isaac missed, our destiny

Pure Heart and Righteous Soul

Timna

Timna – desperate to join the family of the Jews
Would give up being princess, a distinction she would lose
Her motives pure, a righteous soul which was heaven bent
To Abraham to Isaac and to Jacob Timna went
She hoped to marry in this family of nobility
The patriarchs refused converting her, each of the three
The Midrash tells us, we are punished for their grave mistake
A righteous gentile seeking G-d, don't shun, but rather take
As the concubine of Eliphaz, Esau's first son
Bore Amalek our rival sent us from the Holy One
G-d performed great miracles to save us at the sea
The whole world's people shook in fear of their destiny
But Amalek no awe of G-d or fear of Jews, they'd be
The first ones to attack us, let the other nations see
A chink of weakness in the Jews and in the Lord their G-d
To reassess their fear of us and G-d now not so hard
G-d says next time a righteous woman seeks the Holy One
Accept her and embrace her before untold harm is done

Giving

Leah

Leah had six sons, Bilha and Zilpa each had two
Jacob would have only twelve, from prophesy they knew
If the child that Leah carried would be born a son
Her sister Rachel would be relegated to just one
Leah prayed to G-d with all her heart, she did not fail
The embryo within her with G-d's help became female
Instead of seven tribes it seemed just six would come from her
But for her kindness she had part in eight tribes as it were
Her daughter's daughter Asnat married Joseph through
Pharaoh
They had two tribes Menasheh and Ephraim as we know
The kindly act of Leah teaches sometimes that we may
Get much more back than we thought we'd have to give away

Putting Others First

Rachel

Captive Jews thrust from their land, no one to intercede
Except the words of Rachel, G-d did listen to, indeed
Our other sacred ancestors, G-d refused to hear
The special trait Rachel possessed, when we look is quite clear
Throughout her life she suppressed both her wants and needs
She showed that she put others first, with both her words and deeds
She loved Jacob desperately but Laban made him take
Leah for his first wife tricked him into that mistake
But Rachel feared her sister's shame divulged the secret sign
She planned with Jacob, made him think that everything was fine
That wedding night Rachel hid beneath the couple's bed
It wasn't Leah answering – Rachel did instead
Daylight came, the ruse now clear but it was just too late
And to become his cherished wife, Rachel now must wait
Despondent were the seed of Jacob as they passed her way
From the grave her words gave solace as they went away
G-d would bring them back again because of Rachel's deeds
Of putting others first before she took care of her needs

Contribution of the Unknown

Bilhah and Zilpah

Bilhah's and Zilpah's, could it be
Offspring one third of Jewry?
Who were they, what was their claim
To have such status and such fame?
Both of them half-sisters to Leah and Rachael
Companion and close confidants shared in their travail:
Bilhah means "alarmed" to see
That Rachel had no progeny
"Esau, as husband?", Leah cried
As Zilpah also wept and sighed.
When Rachel died, G-d's *schina* went
And moved on top of Bilhah's tent
Indeed, not much more known of them
Except their actions served Hashem
For many years time and again
We recognize and praise the men

But unknown women serve Hashem
As wives and mothers most of them
Their roles may differ from the men
But as important to Hashem
As important, maybe more
For their *neshamot* climb and soar
Compassion, insight within them
Makes them beloved by Hashem

Not Resorting to Lashon Hara

Tamar

This signet, staff and cloak of he
Who brought about my pregnancy
Though she could tell who was to blame
Tamar did not reveal his name
She'd rather burn and lose her life
Than cause another shameful strife
But Judah knew his honesty
Could prevent a travesty
Declaring guilt before all there
Of his sin he was aware
Two sons died, now left with one
So he refused Tamar that son
Her actions to produce a seed
Through Judah righteous, just, indeed
Moshiach's line will come from them
Our ultimate gift from Hashem

Comforter

Serach

"Joseph's alive in Egypt" were the lyrics of her song
Jacob blessed her for these words that's why she lived so long
All the brothers were afraid to offer him this news
They felt his soul was vulnerable, his life they feared he'd lose
But Serach's music comforted, the words he felt were true
It strengthened both his heart and soul; he knew what he
  would do
Serach came to Egypt but she was the only one
Who left alive with Moses when the servitude was done
We see how great the mitzvah is to comfort one in need
And the great reward for Serach who performed this deed

Always Speak the Truth

Asnat

In Egypt Asnat lived with Potifar and with his wife
Once adopted as their daughter, she enjoyed that life
Despite appreciation that she surely owed these two
More important to her was to know and say what's true
Potifar's wife lusted, for Joseph, the young slave
Joseph just ignored her and all the hints she gave
One day, the house thought empty, the two of them alone
She tried seducing Joseph, but he wasn't on his own
The visage of his father he could see before his eyes
He wouldn't sin despite his lust, that caught her by surprise
She grabbed his shirt to later claim he forced himself on her
But unbeknown to both of them, the truth that did occur
Was seen by Asnat, still at home , despite the holiday
She told the truth to Potifar, saved Joseph's life that day
Despite what others do for us and what we may owe them
We must always speak the truth, we speak before Hashem

Expending Effort Brings G-d's Help

Batya, Daughter of Pharoah

From the Nile the lad she drew
And quickly named him Moshe too
His ark at first almost passed by
She stretched her arm to make a try
G-d's miracle made her succeed
Her one effort was all she'd need
She was the daughter of Pharaoh
At first the princess did not know
That he was Hebrew and a Jew
But showed compassion through and through
She took him to her palace home
And raised him as if he were her own
If we make efforts pure and right
G-d too will help with all his might

Belief in Your Prophesy

Miriam

Miriam a female prophet, was extremely wise
At five she knew her father erred, she quickly did surmise
That when he left his wife for fear that they could have a son
Since Pharaoh had decreed sure death for each and every one
She knew that Pharaoh's edict was directed just at males
To leave his wife meant no more daughters so that logic fails
Amram took his wife again, soon had another son
His birth brought joy and light into the house for everyone
But three months later Moses in an ark placed on the Nile
But Miriam of Moses' death was still in great denial
Yocheved upset hit her daughter flush upon her head
But Miriam would not retract the prophesy she said
In her vision, she saw Moses, son to both of them
Lead his people out of bondage following Hashem
Her vindication came the day the Jews crossed the Red Sea
With G-d's help, brother Moses set the Jewish people free

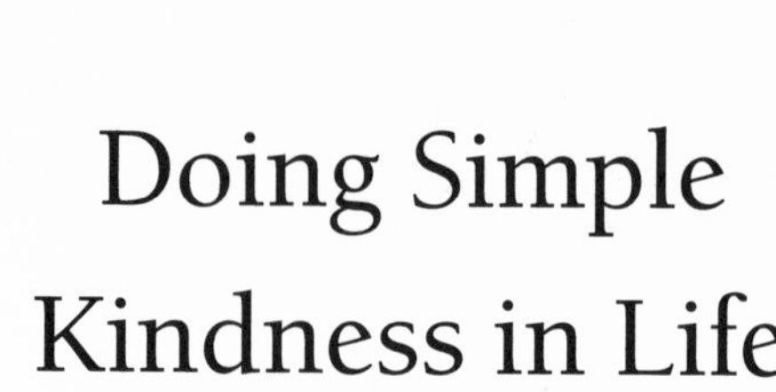

Doing Simple Kindness in Life

Shifra and Puah (Miriam and Yocheved)

Both Shifra and Puah
were midwives of the Jews
They placed all of their faith in G-d,
Their lives they risked to lose
For Pharaoh had commanded
that they kill each Jewish Boy,
Instead they cooed and cleaned each up
with happiness and joy.
From them would issue Kings and Priests,
a blessing from Hashem.
They would see the nation grow,
G-d's second gift to them.
At times the fruits of labor
one may not see in his life,
Just agitation, stress and strain,

tension, risk, and strife
A stunning kindness G-d can give
for all the good we do
Is let us share in our success,
before our days are through.
In truth Shifra and Puah
each had another name
The names Yocheved, Miriam
would merit greater fame
But this proves that Hashem holds dear
the small thing we can do
Simple kindness proves our motives,
mind and heart are true

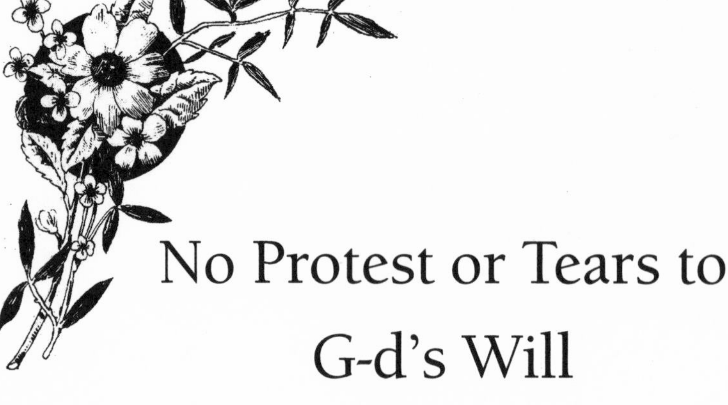

No Protest or Tears to G-d's Will

Elisheva

Could any one have had more pride
Than on the day her two sons died?
Husband Ahron, the High Priest
Elisheva was at least
As proud of her four sons that way
Who served Hashem as priests each day
Grandson Pinchas, Priest of War
And Moses, brother in law
Who served as leader and as King
And brother, Nachshon who would bring
The first day's tribal offering
This day of joy would also bring
True sadness when her two sons die
But she did not protest or cry
She knew G-d has a master plan
And does what's best for every man

Wrong Wife Shattered Life

Korach's Wife

The choice most vital in his life
Is who a man picks for his wife
In the Bible we can see
The wrong wife led to misery
Korach's wife deserves the blame
She drove him to seek status, fame
By claiming self respect he lacked
His worth and manhood she attacked.
In an attempt to please his wife
Korach would forfeit his life
His rift with Moses ill advised
For it was Moses who G-d prized
Swallowed by the earth G-d split.
Korach's grave would be that pit

Protecting a Spouse

Tziporrah

Jethro threw him in a pit
Moses lived ten years in it
Tziporrah sent food down that pit
Though Jethro never knew of it
This way, those years, she saved his life
She'd clearly make a worthy wife
A second time she saved his life
This, when traveling as his wife
To Egypt to help free the Jews
With little time to waste or lose
So Moses held off his son's *bris*
In this G-d felt, he was remiss
G-d sent a snake to swallow him
He disappeared from sight within
Tziporrah quickly took a flint
Cut the foreskin and by dint
Of this, the snake let Moses go
Her swift, smart actions clearly show
Her bridegroom Moses kept alive
Her son's *bris* blood let him survive

Finding Value in the Holy Land

The Daughters of Zelaphechad
(Mahlah, Noah, Haglah, Milcah, Tirzah)

Zelaphechad died without a son
His five daughters were gems, each one
The land of Israel they did prize
That's why the Rabbis called them wise
Biding time, they said no word
Until from Moses' mouth they heard
The laws of *yibum* that he taught
And questioned him with this retort:
Our father died without a son
Let our mother marry one
Who can inherit father's land
And keep it in our family's hand
He said, "*yibum* she can not do,
Your father had the five of you"
They said, "If this is truly so.

To us five, the land must go
If we prevent the *yibum* rite
To share his land should be our right"
Moses knew not of this law
No case like this had come before.
The Lord said that their words were just
Right then Moses knew that he must
Teach this new law in their name
And so their wisdom grew in fame

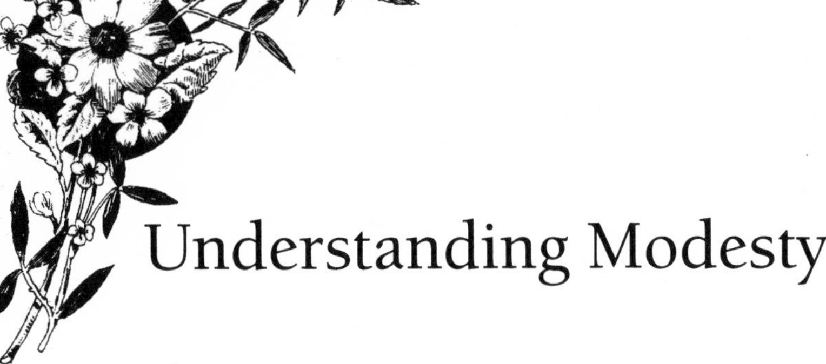

Understanding Modesty

Jewish Wives in Egypt

Jewish slaves no time for rest
In heart and soul they were depressed
Afflicted in both body, soul
Just to survive became their goal
Both tired, without energy
No strength was left for progeny
But since this meant that they could face
The possible end of our race
The wives primp by a looking glass
Of copper, so their men won't pass
But be enticed to procreate
This godly act, assured our fate
To prove their's was the purest deed
Despite how they did intercede
The women's copper mirrors' place
Became the laver top to base
That's where the Cohen washes hands
To make them pure as G-d commands

Anticipating G-d's Glory

Jewish Woman at the Red Sea

The women more attuned than men
Expected wonders from Hashem
In Egypt with the plagues they saw
At the Red Sea looked for more
They came with cymbals, tambourines
To praise G-d's supernatural means
First, he split the sea in two
A path for Israel to pass through
So Egypt could not capture them
The water raised back by Hashem
Egyptians were drowned one by one
Before G-d's miracle was done
To praise Hashem, men sang each word
From women music also heard
The women ready and prepared
To praise G-d since they planned and cared

A Special Holiday for Women

Each new moon is a holiday
Our women free from work that day
It is a gift from G-d above
To thank them for their faith and love
For when in Egypt we were slaves
Just sleep and rest a body craves
Depressed, without the energy
To reproduce with progeny
We risked extinction, had no hope
But Jewish wives knew how to cope
Enticed the men to procreate
Their G-dly act assured our fate
To make the golden calf refused
To give their gold, so were abused
With slurs and anger from the men
Who seized gold jewelry from them

The Tabernacle for Hashem
To build, they came before men
To offer up their silver , gold
For when it's built, they were told
G-d's eminence would come to stay
Remain with us there every day
The women gave with faith and trust
To serve Hashem they felt they must
So why a new moon holiday
For them? So G-d could clearly say,
"As moonlight in the dark brings hope
Their faith in G-d helped us all cope".

Women Got the Torah Before the Men

So cherished were they by Hashem
He gave the Torah first to them
The women first and then the men
Then in time to their children
The first concept of a G-d
Invisible, for children hard
When love of Torah mothers teach
A sense of G-d is within reach
Instill some Torah, the next goal
To place that spirit in their soul
And finally would come the love
For Hashem who reigns above
Not tainted by the calf of gold
Their faith in G-d was their stronghold
Who better to prepare a soul
To G-d than righteous wives of old
That's why it was planned by Hashem
To give the Torah first to them

MIRACLE WORKER

Wife of Ohn Ben Pellis

Ohn Ben Pellis had a wife
Who absolutely saved his life
Absented him from Korach's fight
With Moses who was in the right
She sat before their open tent
When for Ohn some men were sent
No hat or cover on her head
Ohn inside was drunk in bed
The men were modest stayed outside
Then went away while Ohn did hide
the Israelites saw wrath from G-d
Korach's judgement swift and hard
First burned, then he fell through the ground
But Ohn was not there to be found
Although Ohn's tent, began to tilt
His wife prayed, so G-d cleansed his guilt
A miracle did save Ohn's life
That miracle was his wise wife

Women in the Prophets and Megilot

Awe of G-d

Rahab

One who says a lie based
on his awe of G-d, the Lord
Inherits life in two worlds,
as was Rahab's just reward
She told the King of Jericho
two spies had fled, but lied
Instead she took them to her roof
where they could safely hide
For forty years she lived a life
of sin, she did not know
About G-d great and powerful,
until her soul did grow,
The rope the lamp and window
many years had sinned with them
Became the objects of repentance
as she served Hashem
Joshua would marry her
and when we read the prayer

Aleinu that her husband wrote
we see her presence there
" G-d above in heaven
and on earth below"
She said to prove her faith in G-d
so that the spies would know
From her would issue priest
and prophets, also her reward
We see how much a "lie for awe"
is cherished by the Lord

Faith in Elders

Yiftach's daughter

Her father's blunders were to blame
Their impact, her faith overcame
As general he made a vow
If G-d helps me to prevail now
Against my evil foes in war
The first to greet me at my door
I'll sacrifice to you, my Lord
This oath he felt he could afford
For he thought that his dog would be
The first one at the door he'd see
His daughter came first to the door
His vow though, he could not ignore
There is no human offering
Kosher livestock one must bring
Pinchas could annul his vow
But Yiftach was too haughty now
"first let Pinchas come to me
For I produced a victory"

Some say she went to mountain tops
Her ban on marriage could not stop
The Medrash says the mountains were
Great Elders who might find for her
A way to void the vow, so she
Could live her life as meant to be

Pure Faith

Manoach's wife

Manoach, Samson's father,
was not a learned man
His wife came from Judea,
He from the tribe of Dan
She, a righteous woman
without daughter, without son
She knew her only hope
Was to entreat the Holy One
She prayed with fervor and G-d's angel
came and said she'd see
A son with might, a Nazirite,
and judge for Jewry
He'd be a holy Nazirite,
G-d's miracle from birth
A further attestation
of his mother's stellar worth
She followed all instructions
that the angel gave to her

Her preparations for this child
did perfectly concur
The simple man Manoach
did not merit such a son
It was his wife's pure faith
and all the praying she had done

Praying With the Heart

Chana

Chana had no children
so she prayed to G-d, the Lord
He answered her prayer to him,
that was her just reward
When she came to the Temple,
she saw no one around
But Eli the high priest was there
and soon she would be found
He saw her lips were moving
And at first her prayer seemed fine
But since he heard no sound,
he thought she had been drinking wine
Her actions were quite proper
and the model how to pray
We say our *Shmoneh Esrei*
silently that way
And that child that she prayed for
to Hashem so very hard
Was Samuel, the prophet
sent forth to her by G-d

Picking Up the Pieces

Naomi

Coming back to Bethlehem
Left with her spouse and two sons when
A famine struck the Holy Land
No sustenance or food at hand
She left and felt fulfilled in life
A mother and a cherished wife
Her three men, leaders of the Jews
The people found it hard to lose
These men's support and leadership
When hardships came, they jumped ship
Their decision angered G-d
His punishment was swift and hard
The three died very far from home
And left Naomi all alone
Except for Ruth her dead son's wife
She felt she faced an empty life
Naomi did miscalculate
She bemoaned her current fate

In truth no one of us can know
The kindness that Hashem will show
In time to G-d in joy she'll sing
She'll see from Ruth comes David, King
Eventually Moshiach, too
A kindness that Hashem will do
We too must hope and contemplate
'Til G-d sends him we pray and wait

Loyalty

Ruth

"Wherever you go I'll go too
And to your faith, I will be true.
Where you lodge and eat, I'll dine,
Your G-d and people will be mine."
Ruth had wed Naomi's son
Though he was dead, she'd be the one
To help Naomi, times were bad
And not leave her as Orpah had.
Her logic hard to understand
She was a princess in her land.
Instead of opulence at home
Naomi she'd not leave alone
Her dedication not too hard
To be recognized by G-d
For her loyalty and concern
A great reward in time she'd earn
From her line comes David, King
Moshiach too, who G-d will bring

Keep Climbing in G-dliness

Ruth and Orpah

Ruth married Naomi's son
Orpah wed the other one
Both sons died, Naomi grieved
G-d's punishment her sons received
She left Moav, returning home
To Bethlehem, was not alone
Ruth and Orpah came along
Naomi feared they'd not belong
Naomi first tried to dissuade
Them from the plans that they made
Orpah listened, Ruth said, "No
Wherever you go, I will go"
Since she ignored Naomi's plea
One day Boaz's wife she'd be
From them would come David, King
While to the world, Orpah would bring

Goliath, evil, crude and vile
Who victimized Jews quite a while
In truth, Orpah was not so bad
With kindly loyalty she had
Joined Naomi on her way
'Til she was told ,"return, don't stay"
Ask why Goliath comes from her
A decent woman as it were
She had the chance her soul could soar
Be close to G-d forever more
But when she left Naomi's side
A downward spiral she would ride
When our spirit yearns to grow
In G-dliness we have to know
Keep climbing upward do not stall
When you stop, you start to fall

Kindness

The Shunamite Woman

Abishag the Shunamite
had a sister of great fame
So prominent a women,
yet we do not know her name
Thoughtful kind, and generous,
this was her giving way
And those who give most graciously,
G-d will reward one day
Elisha, judge and prophet,
At times traveled through the land
She opened up her home to him
and opened up her hand
Made a little chamber
on the roof where he could live
With bed and light and table,
she thought not that much to give
One day her son fell in the field
and could not take a breath

Couldn't get up from the ground,
seemed very close to death
Then Elisha blew in breath
Life came back to her son
A power that was given to him
by the Holy One
In truth, the mother's kindness
had earned this great reward
For kindness pays back kindness,
this the way of our Lord
The son her acts of kindness saved,
his name was Habakkuk
Who prophesized to Israel,
says the holy Zohar Book

Jewish Woman of War

Devorah

Devorah made thick wicks
so that the temple's lights would shine
Her olive trees made olive oil,
her orchards made fine wine
Modestly, a judge who taught
The Torah of Hashem
Sat beneath a palm in sight,
Did not seclude with men
But when the battle came
she led the Jews to victory
Then she praised the Lord Hashem,
with songs and poetry

Jewish Woman of War

Yael

Sisera the General
escaped the fray and ran
Since he didn't realize
no one can thwart G-d's plan
He thought that he was free and clear,
ran into Yael's tent
The righteous Yael understood
at once why he was sent
To slake his thirst she gave him milk
and then put him into bed
And when asleep she rammed
the tent pin right into his head

Jewish Woman of War

Yehudis

Greek king Holofornes
planned to take Jerusalem
If not for brave Yehudis
who before he did, would come
Beautiful and cunning
and the daughter of a priest
Brought him food in a bag
and promised him a feast
As Yael did with Sisera
first fed him salty cheese
Then offered him a jug of wine
to satisfy and please
When he fell asleep from wine
she quickly cut his head
This vile and evil King of Greece,
Through her act was now dead
The troops still poised and ready,
just waiting to invade
She showed them all their leader's head,
they ran away afraid

Choosing Truth

Michal

When a daughter's father errs,
what is she to do?
Should she still support him
with his words and acts untrue?
King Saul was Michal's father,
hoped to end young David's life
Said," Kill a hundred Philistines
receive a princess wife"
He hoped for David's failure
and his death in the attempt
But when young David did succeed,
Saul just had contempt
Later in the palace Michal
heard the plans to kill
David, now betrothed to her,
It was her father's will
She helped him through a window
to escape her father's wrath

An angry Saul wed her
to Paltiel, the aftermath.
But betrothed to David
she could wed no other man
With Paltiel not intimate,
As per the Torah's ban
A sword beside them in the bed,
warned them not to sin
For humankind has passion,
which starts quickly from within
Paltiel left. Michal in time
became King David's spouse
She chose a truthful husband,
rather than her father's house

Beauty and Wisdom

Abigail

One of four, most beautiful
that mankind ever knew
One of seven women
who were known as prophets too
Abigail was clearly fit
to be a queen, it's true
Yet, it was her wisdom
that King David was drawn to.
He planned to hold his court
convicting Nabal in the night
She said night judgments by our laws
are not considered right
David said I execute
all rebels that they bring
"most", she said, "think not you
but that Saul is still the king"
The Talmud said her words
protected King David from sin

No sacrifice, if he killed Nabal
would atone for him
Of all the women David knew
or met throughout his life
Abigail, the wisest,
David picked to be his wife

Anticipates the Future

Batsheva

Batsheva, David's Queen,
was truly meant to be his wife
It's obvious when we hear
this story in her life
When the first child they conceived,
died, she made David swear
That if they had another son,
King David would declare
That son one day would follow him
as the Jewish King
No matter what the benefits
other sons could bring
The years passed by and David weak,
was lying on his bed
The prophet Nathan came,
reminded her, and then he said,
"Now's the time with oath and promise
King David be bound

To name the next King – Solomon
to all those now around".
She approached the King,
thereby brought kingship to her son
But also served the will and plan
of G-d, the Holy One.
Who gave this man so sensitive
the wisdom he would need
To lead the people properly
as king in thought and deed

Finding our Bashert

Solomon's Daughter

A daughter was the favorite child
of Solomon the King
Indeed he loved her more
than anyone or anything
A peasant scribe asked Solomon
for her hand to wed
This precious daughter he refused
and planned to hide instead
He sent her to an island
which was far across the sea
She was protected in a tower,
hidden secretly
The scribe crestfallen, sad and crying,
was in deep despair
Got drunk with wine, the pain of losing her
too much to bear
Felt cold while in a stupor
sleeping drunk upon the ground.
Then crawled into a carcass
nearby him that he had found
A bird of prey directed there
then swooped down from the sky

Scooped up the scribe and carcass
in its beak and still could fly
Across the sea for hours flew
then landed in the place
The princess was, a miracle
clearly by G-d's grace.
The princess saw him in the garden
knew him from before
But the tower had been locked
No entry through the door
From the steeple where she was
she let down her long hair
He climbed up through the window,
to join his beloved there
Professed to her his feelings
and declared to her his love
Both were sure their union
was the plan of G-d above
The King upon his visit
was confused and wondered why
From the tower steeple
He could hear a baby cry
Then he saw his daughter
who had wed the peasant scribe
He did not even scream or shout
or rant a diatribe.
Instead he laughed for now he knew
It was G-d's will that won
Man has plans, but all are subject
to the Holy One

Soft Chastisement

Hulda

In Lamentations Jeremiah
prophesized despair
The fall of Old Jerusalem,
most Jews exiled from there
Jeremiah had a cousin –
and Hulda was her name
For acts of kindness at the gates
her husband had gained fame
He gave out drinks of water
to those thirsty he would see
And for that merit, his wife Hulda,
heard G-d's prophesy
King Josiah didn't call her cousin
but called her
For women, Softer, show compassion,
mercy as it were
Words of rebuke, retribution
said for heaven's sake

When couched in euphemistic terms
are easier to take
Words sometimes rejected because
of anger they provoke
Her's accepted by the king
and people when she spoke
Jeremiah's words of fire, brimstone,
were not heard
Hulda's soft chastisement,
people listened to her word

Unwavering Faith

Hannah

Antiochus made decrees
That all Jews bow and bend their knees
Before an idol placed near them
To show they lost faith in Hashem
Hannah and her seven sons
Were martyrs each and every one
Would not bow to a god of stone
Just to the one true G-d alone
Each son in turn, was warned he'd lose
His life, but each did still refuse
To reject G-d and be set free
No chance he'd choose idolatry
As she saw each son lose his life
All could feel her pain and strife
But still encouraged every son
To love and fear the Holy One
And before the youngest died
Tearful but with mother's pride

Said, "When you see Abraham
Tell him that with faith I am
Offering G-d all my sons
While he asked you for only one,
But when I saw your faith in G-d
I offered seven though quite hard."

Queen Esther

Fast Prayers and Action

We all dress up on Purim day
To publicize G-d's role that way
Our costumes hide identity
G-d hid his, but set us free
Most every female child in shul
Dresses by the simple rule
Look like Esther, queen, that night
Who spotting danger set things right
For Esther took on center stage
To counter Haman's hate and rage
Her fast and praying made him lose
In his attempt to kill the Jews
But Esther did not merely pray
She risked her life for Jews that day
Without consent came to the king
This was quite a risky thing
But Achashvarosh loved the queen
And promised her that it would mean

That he'd arrange on her behalf
Divide his kingdom, give her half
We see the story ebb and flow
As Esther urged the king to know
How vicious, tasteless, cruel and mean
Haman was against the Queen
Then Hamen really lost his head
He climbed right in to Esther's bed
To beg her that she spare his life
The king thought Haman craved his wife
And finally we clearly see
G-d punishes with irony
The tree meant to hang Mordechai
Instead hung Hamen very high
The Jews realized, it wasn't hard
That in the background it was G-d
Who quietly devised the plan
To save each woman, child and man
Appreciating what was done
Each year we thank The Holy One

Choosing the Wrong Wife

Jezebel

King Ahab's wife was Jezebel
Because of her from grace he fell
She prayed to idols not to G-d
But still Ahab found it too hard
From her spell to break away
He greatly angered G-d this way
Despite the many times G-d sent
A chance for Ahab to repent
Jezebel blocked his return
His punishment not her concern
The man appointed Israel's king
Despite his downfall chose to cling
To Jezebel his evil wife
It cost Ahab eternal life

Women in the Talmud

Charity Saves From Death

Rabbi Akiva's Daughter

Astrologers look upwards,
tell the futures from the stars
Predict the fates of nations,
of others, not of ours.
Although when read correctly,
predictions can be true
But we can overcome them
with our prayers and good deeds too
Before his daughter's wedding,
Rav Akiva heard it said
The stars do clearly tell us
that tomorrow she'll be dead
By daylight the next morning,
he found her safe and sound
She then revealed a dead snake
from her room that she had found

The night before a pauper
came looking for some food
The others were quite busy,
ignored him and were rude
But she had true compassion
Gave to him her food to eat
One single act of kindness,
her redemption was complete

Making One's Husband a Talmud Chacham

Rachel (Rabbi Akiva's Wife)

It's told Rabbi Akiva
had a very special wife
A husband who learned Torah,
Was the essence of her life
Her father was quite wealthy,
she could live in luxury
But chose to wed Akiva
for the sage that he could be
In time he left her and his home
to learn for twelve full years
Comes finally to see her,
but just as he appears
Her back to him, she says ,
"today he comes a learned man"
Should he ask for twelve more years
I'd tell him that he can
With these words heard,

Akiva left, to her he didn't speak
Went back to learn G-d's Talmud,
as its jewels and gems he'd seek

Seeing The Essence of Things

Bruria *(Rabbi Meir's Wife)*

There was a disbeliever
that the Talmud calls a "*min*".
His silly questions to Rav Meir
wore his patience thin
Rav Meir one day prayed to G-d
to end this doubter's life
That was until he heard stern words
from Bruria his wife
G-d wants the end of sin itself,
not the sinner's life
"pray that he repents not dies ",
said Bruria his wife
Rav Meir finally saw his wife
as "*azer kinegdo*"
Though a Torah giant
until then he did not know

Value of Torah Study

Daughter of "Acher"

When all man's days on earth are gone
His memory can carry on
Through his Torah and his deeds
Or a child who intercedes
Elisha fell from grace to shame
"Acher" then became his name
Doubted G-d's complete control
And in the world his daily role
As for children, he had one
A single daughter, but no son
She came to Rebbi with this plea,
"Please open up your hand, help me"
My father's Torah, learned, should stand
Although his deeds you reprimand
A fire came where Rebbi stood
Burned his lectern, so he would
See that Torah without deed
Still had a worth itself indeed

Immediate Chesed

Choni Hamagel's Wife

Choni stood inside a circle,
uttered this refrain:
Dear G-d, I will stand right here
until you make it rain
One time there was no rainfall
with the plight extremely bad
This time no use for circles
though in the past he had,
Choni called his wife instead
to pray on their roof top
Each stood in his own corner
and neither one would stop
Until thick laden rain clouds
appeared into their clear view
All those there were quite surprised,
a bit bewildered too......
No clouds appeared above his head,
but were above his wife's instead

Choni not a bit surprised,
It was her chesed that G-d prized
The poor she brought into her home
Ate right away, and not alone
For charity without delay
The rain clouds first would come her way
Instead of Choni's old refrain
This time her chesed brought the rain

A Mother's Love

The High Priest's Mother

When one killed another by accident
To the city of refuge by the court he was sent
Continually forced to stay there each day
Until the time came – the High Priest passed away
Then he'd go home to his family and wife
And try to regain and restart his old life
When someone was stuck there day after day
It's likely eventually he'd start to pray
For freedom and that the High Priest pass away
To finally end this long imposed stay
Even a sinner's prayers at times will count
But only with true, heartfelt words coming out
But if prayers are weak, lacking intensity
They never will merit the Lord's full mercy
Knowing the truth in this to save a son
To the cities of refuge mothers had begun
To bring all the inmates cakes, drinks and sweets
Clothing, fine foods, and other nice treats
This blunted the sharp edge of pain when they pray
To G-d that her son, the High Priest, pass away

Kindness Through Personal Effort

Mar Ukvah's Wife

Mar Ukvah and his wife were
very generous and kind
To help but not embarrass others
foremost in their mind
They'd bring food to the needy,
but when no one was around
To spare humiliation
In case they would be found
One day they brought cooked food
to feed a needy family
Once inside the house,
within the garden they could see
The family was returning,
in just moments would be there
The two were not expecting this,
had no time to prepare

Both hid in a large oven
so that they would not be found
And though the oven's floor was hot,
they couldn't chance a sound
Mar Ukvah's feet were singed,
but his wife's feet remained just fine,
His students asked him if this was
a sign from the Divine
Mar Ukvah said," her efforts great,
to cook and to prepare
I only earned the money
and helped her bring food there
Part of kindness is the effort that
our body makes
And G-d repays us for the effort
that each kindness takes

A Woman of Valor Yesterday and Today

Solomon's Woman of Valor

(*Proverbs* 31:10-31)

A woman of valor is worth more than pearls
When her man's heart trusts in her, his fortune prevails
Her acts will not harm him, just generate good
With gladness spins linen and wool as she should
Like a far away ship bringing its bounty home
Prepares for her household early morning alone..
From the sale of her handiwork buys her own field,
Then planting her vineyard, brings her family its yield
Girds her body with mitzvot which strengthen her arm
Sees all her work G-dly, this is part of her charm
Works by the candle at night, not in bed
Her palm on the spindle, stretches wool into thread
Opens her hand up giving alms to the poor
For snow in her wool garb, her household secure
Makes bedspreads and clothing in royal purple and blue
Worn by her husband distinctively too

As he sits by the gates near those famed in the land
Her cloaks and her belts all the peddlers demand
Majestic, with power knows her last day brings joy
Her tongue and her mouth, kindness, wisdom employ
The needs of her household she knows from the start
From the bread of the idle, she never takes part
Her children all praise her, her husband does, too
Many daughters of Jacob have flourished, it's true
But you have surpassed all, their beauty and grace
A G-d fearing woman no one else can replace
Grant her the fruits of her hands that she needs
And let her be praised at the gates for her deeds

A Modern Day Woman of Valor

A woman of valor who exists in these days
Is worthy of accolades, sweet words of praise
Wakes up in the morning before the day's light
Prepares for her household so all things go right
First packs the lunch bags, then sets clothes out for school
Starts cooking breakfast, before seven the rule
Drops off her kids at Yeshiva by eight
Then to her workplace without being late
Her job is to help pay tuition and rent
It's hard to believe how fast money is spent
When she comes home, she sees that the youngest has flu
After the doctor, there is shopping to do
Then chauffeurs her children to sports practice too
Prepares gourmet dinners as if nothing to do
Sends off her husband after dinner to learn
While he's in shul for her chores still remain

Then helps with homework or does washing instead
By now she is tired and craves sleeping in bed
But still there is ironing and buttons to sew
When her husband comes home she has duties, you know
With a G-d fearing woman picked as his wife
A man can have an incredible life
Her soul guides her actions, her heart guides her hands
And both are upholding the Torah's commands
And in her old age, she's still lover and friend
Can't think of a better way for life to end

The Mitzvah and Segulah of Lighting Candles

When woman light on Friday night
Their candles bring the Shabbas light
And as they kindle women pray
To G-d and with great hope they say,

"May I merit from Hashem
That my offspring have in them
Torah knowledge and are wise
Awe and love of G-d they prize
Men of truth, so pure a seed
Being close to G-d their need
With Torah learning light the Earth
Good deeds and G-d's work as their worth"

Their candles shine so pure and bright
So it seems quite just and right
That worthy children come from them
Who through their acts will serve Hashem

When You Kindle Sabbath Light

With your family Friday night
Pray to G-d with all your might
That he should render all wrongs, right
To bring his people joy and health
Peace and goodness, blessings, wealth
He waits all week to hear your prayer
When you light, he is there

Woman's Mitzvah

Tithing Bread

The Talmud says a man's success
Is based on his wife's worthiness
If caring, charitable and kind
Her husband is most sure to find
That he is sustained by the Lord
Which is in truth his wife's reward
Accordingly it's quite correct
That she takes tithes and not neglect
That mitzvah from the things she bakes
Bread, matzah, and challah cakes
But in these days when we're not sure
Which lines of Cohanim are pure
We cannot give these tithes away
Until, G-d willing, see the day
Moshiach comes, the Temple stands
Again give tithes as G-d commands
But taking tithes still has a place
Among frum women, commonplace

When young, this omen helps them catch
Their bashert, their G-d sent match
They also helps to bring the cure
For those with illness or those poor
The Talmud calls man's wife, his bread
Since to the staff of life he's wed

Women and the Mitzvah of Shofar

Women took upon themselves
to hear the Shofar sound
Although it's time dependent,
and therefore they're not bound
Perhaps because it elevates
their spirit and their soul
Spurs them on to emulate
G-d as their chosen goal
Like G-d they are creators
bringing life to mankind too
Sustain, and nourish embryos
until their time is due
Just like G-d, their mercy
shines through all the good they do
Their kindness is apparent,
their judgments fair and true

When G-d created humans
with a single breath he'd give
Spirit to both soul and body,
not just air to live
The breath that G-d once gave men,
blowing shofar they return
To show it's used for good deeds
and for Torah they can learn
Women listen to the Shofar's
Sound so G-d will know
His breath that gave them life,
gave spirit, so their souls could grow

Segula...Sending Away the Mother Bird

When a kosher mother bird is sitting on her nest
To protect her eggs and chicks, she does her very best
There is a Torah law to take the chicks but shoo the bird
About this law there is special segulah that we've heard
Women without children or who want to have a son
Why of all the mitzvot are they told to do this one ?
When the mother bird comes back her anguish has begun
The nest is empty void of eggs of chicks, not even one.
We see maternal love and caring even from a bird
"I'd do much more for my offspring" would be the woman's word
The fact that instinct caused the bird to love reminds Hashem
How women love their children, no bird can compete with them

At the Wedding

Seven times the Kallah makes
a circle 'round her spouse'
To prove she'll build a worthy
Torah home within their house
And that her Chassan will become
the center of her life
In turn her husband will provide
and love his cherished wife
As walls of Jericho when circled
fell the seventh time
So barriers between them will fall
throughout their whole lifetime
And if they always feel the joy
they felt their wedding day
A happy life together,
serving G-d is on its way.

Four Cups Of Wine at the Seder

Each woman at the Seder
must drink four cups of wine
If she possesses stature,
she also must recline
The Talmud in Pesachim
tells us this must be
It was in part their righteous acts
for why G-d set us free
Never intermarried,
served their husbands faithfully
Observed the laws of mikvah
and of family purity
At times they slaved with rigor,.
Like the men worked very hard
But never lost full faith
Of the redemption by their G-d

Kept their Hebrew language,
Hebrew name and modest clothes
Proud of who they were, stood out,
so everybody knows
Now they recline drinking wine,
not simply being free
But since G-d brought us freedom
by dint of their piety

Segula of Saying Perek Shira for Forty Days

Our women do say Perek Shira
Forty days as a *segula*
When they do G-d can arrange
To bring into their lives a change
The soul mate they are looking for
A child. Their health, new wealth and more
Why forty days grant such rewards?
The standard set up is the lord's :
The embryo 'til thirty-nine
Like water, of no clear design
But at forty days, a life
A *bat kol* calls out who's his wife
In the days of Noah's ark
Evil made the world turn dark
For forty days rain washed away
The whole world's sins a bit each day

A forty *seh* pool made of rain
Impurity will not remain
When we submerge the body, whole
This way G-d helps to cleanse our soul
Why Perek Shira grants reward?
In it all recognize the Lord
His praises each creation sings
And thereby lauds the King of Kings
We say their words of praise then can
Understand the role of man

Sources

16 • **ABOUT WOMEN AND ANGELS**
Shasani kirzono – made me according to his (G-d's) will.
neshamas – souls

18 • **THE BEAUTY OF G-D'S OWN HAND** — *EVE*
Brachos 61a, Osios d'Rabbi Akiva Atbash
Gen 2:22, Avos d'Rabbi Nosson 4:3

19 • **BRING PLEASANTNESS TO THE WORLD** — *NAAMAH*
Bereishis Rabba 23:3, Targum Yonasan Bereshis 4:22,
Naamah means pleasant

20 • **BINAH** — *SARAH*
Binah – intuition
Bereishis Rabba 53:13, Gen21:12 (and Rashi)

21 • **THE RIGHTEOUS FALL INTO THE RIGHT PATH** — *LOT'S DAUGHTERS*
Talmud Nazir 21a Although a 'noahide' was allowed to marry his daughter, this was not commonplace and thought distasteful. Lot's daughters' motives were pure and they were rewarded by being forbearers of the Moshiach (Messiah)

22 • **FAITHFUL TO A MATE** — *HAGAR*
Lekach Tov Bereishis 25, Gen 25:1 Rashi

23 • **CARRY ON TRADITION** — *REBECCA*
Gen 24:67, Rashi
When G-d visited Rebecca with the three miracles, Sarah enjoyed during her lifetime, Isaac knew Rebecca was meant to be his wife

24 • **RECOGNIZING OUR PEOPLE'S DESTINY** — *REBECCA*
Bereishis Rabba 65:10, Genesis 25:23, and chapter 27

26 • **PURE HEART AND RIGHTEOUS SOUL** — *TIMNA*
Sanhedrin 99B

27 • **GIVING** — *LEAH*
Genesis 30:21, Bereishis Rabba 72:6, Talmud Berachos 60a and Megillah 13b
Gen. 41:45, When Joseph was appointed Viceroy, Pharaoh assigned Asnat to marry him

28 • **PUTTING OTHERS FIRST** — *RACHEL*
Pesikta Echai Rabbasi 24, Talmud Megillah 13b, Bereshis Rabba 82:10 and 74:4-5,

29 • **CONTRIBUTION OF THE UNKNOWN** — *BILHAH AND ZILPAH*
Schina – G-d's eminence Neshamot-souls

Sechel Tov: Torah Sheleimah 82 (brought in Artscroll Tanach series — Vayetzeh)
Zohar 1:17

31 • **NOT RESORTING TO LASHON HARA** — *TAMAR*
Gen. chapter 38, Zohar 1:888b

32 • **COMFORTER** — *SERACH*
Pirkei d'Rebi Eliezer, Shemos Rabba 5:13
Serach informed Jacob the Joseph was still alive in Egypt with a comforting song.

33 • **ALWAYS SPEAK THE TRUTH** — *ASNAT*
Yalkut Shimoni Vayeishiv 146, Talmud Yoma 35b, Bereishis Rabba 87:5, Talmud Sotah 36b

34 • **EXPENDING EFFORT BRINGS G-D'S HELP** — *BATYA*
Talmud Sotah 12b

35 • **BELIEF IN YOUR PROPHESY** — *MIRIAM*
Talmud Megillah 14a ,Talmud Sotah 12a, Shemos Rabba 1:22

36 • **DOING SIMPLE KINDNESS IN LIFE** — *SHIFRA and PUAH*
Ex 1:15-20 called Shifra for making the babies clean and beautiful, Puah for cooing with them (see Rashi)

38 • **NO PROTEST OR TEARS TO G-D'S WILL** — *ELISHEVA*
Talmud Zevachim 102a

39 • **WRONG WIFE SHATTERED LIFE** — *KORACH'S WIFE*
Sanhedrin 110a

40 • **PROTECTING A SPOUSE** — *TZIPORRAH*
Targum Yonasan Shemos 2:21, Yalkut Shimoni, Shemos 168
Ex 4;25 Shemos Rabba 5:8, Zohar 1:93b
Bris – circumcision

41 • **FINDING VALUE IN THE HOLY LAND** —
THE DAUGHTERS OF ZELAPHECHAD
Yibum – Levirate marriage, Num 27:1-11 Talmud Baba Basra119b

47 • **WOMEN GOT THE TORAH BEFORE THE MEN**
Genesis 9:3 G-d first instructs Moses to tell the Torah to *Bais Yakov* (the women) and then to *Benai Yiroel* (the men)

50 • **AWE OF G-D** — *RAHAB*
Talmud Zevachim 116b Megilah 14b Josh 2
(The words in the prayer Aleinu..."God above in heaven and on earth below" are in the Torah but were also said by Rahab [Josh2] to the spies to show her faith in Hashem. When Joshua wrote this prayer he may very well have added these exact words in deference to his wife Rahab

52 • **FAITH IN ELDERS** — *YIFTACH'S DAUGHTER*
Bereshis Rabba 60:3, Shemos Rabba 1

54 • **PURE FAITH** — *MANOACH'S WIFE*
Judges chapter 13 Tzemach Hashem LaTzvi
(quoted by "Early Prophets" Mesorah Press

56 • **PRAYING WITH THE HEART** — **CHANA**
1 Samuel Chapter 1

57 • **PICKING UP THE PIECES** — *NAOMI*
Megillah of Ruth Chapter 1

59 • **LOYALTY** — *RUTH*
Megillah of Ruth Chapter 1 and 4

60 • **KEEP CLIMBING IN G-DLINESS** — *RUTH AND ORPAH*
Megillah of Ruth chapter 1, Ruth Rabba 2:20

62 • **KINDNESS** — *THE SHUNAMITE WOMAN*
Abishag was King David's attendant at the end of his life,
ll Kings 4:25, Zohar 1:7b and 2:44a, Talmud Brachos 10b
Pirkei d'Rabbi Eliezer 33

64 • **JEWISH WOMAN OF WAR** — *DEVORAH*
Judges 4:4,5 Rashi Talmud Megillah 14a

65 • **JEWISH WOMAN OF WAR** — *YAEL*
Judges chapter 5

66 • **JEWISH WOMAN OF WAR** — *YEHUDIS*
Different accounts identify Holofornes as either King or General

67 • **CHOOSING TRUTH** — *MICHAL*
Sanhedrin 19b, Shocher Tov 59:1

69• **BEAUTY AND WISDOM** — *ABIGAIL*
l Samuel chapter 25, Talmud Megilah 14 a,b, 15a

71 • **ANTICIPATES THE FUTURE** — *BATSHEVA*
ll Samuel 12:15-19,24, Kings 1:11,12,17

73 • **FINDING OUR BASHERT** — *SOLOMON'S DAUGHTER*
Medrash Tanhuma S.Buber ed intro pg68

75 • **SOFT CHASTISEMENT** — *HULDA*
Talmud Megilah 14a,b, Pirkei d'Rabbi Eliezer 33

79 • **QUEEEN ESTHER** — *FAST PRAYERS AND ACTION*
Megilah of Esther

84 • **CHARITY** — *RABBI AKIVA'S DAUGHTER*
Talmud Shabbas 156b

86 • **MAKING ONE'S HUSBAND A TALMUD CHACHAM** — *RACHEL*
Talmud Nedarim 50a

88 • **SEEING THE ESSENCE OF THINGS** — *BRURIA*
Talmud Berachos 10a
azer kenegdo – an advisor

89 • **VALUE OF TORAH STUDY** — *DAUGHTER OF "ACHER"*
Elisha ben Abuyah became a disbeliever when he saw a child fall to his death after performing both commandments of honoring his father's wishes) and sending away the mother bird. Both of these commandments guarantee a long life. Elisha's daughter, probably with the prayer for Grace in mind approached Rebbi (Rabbi Judah, the Prince and President of the Sanhedrin) asking for help. The Prayer for Grace states that a righteous man's children never starve. Her contention was that that father's Torah learning qualified him as righteous even though his deeds were lacking. When a fire from heaven struck Rebbi's table, he said,"If this is on account of one who studies but dishonors Torah, how much more for one who studies and honors it." See Talmud Chagiga 15b

90 • **IMMEDIATE CHESED** — *CHONI HAMAGEL'S WIFE*
Talmud Taanit 23b
chesed- kindness

92 • **A MOTHER'S LOVE** — *THE HIGH PRIEST'S MOTHER*
Makkot Mishna 2:6

93 • **KINDNESS THROUGH PERSONAL EFFORT** — *MAR UKVAH'S WIFE*
Talmud Ketuvos 67b

100 • **THE MITZVAH AND SEGULAH OF LIGHTING CANDLES**
Segulah – good omen

102 • **WOMAN'S MITZVAH** — *TITHING BREAD*
Frum – religious
Bashert – soul mate

111 • **SEGULAH OF SAYING PEREK SHIRA FORTY DAYS**
Seh – biblical liquid measure, about 200 gallons
Bat Kol – voice from heaven

DEDICATED BY ALL THE

ARYEH CHILDREN
and GRANDCHILDREN

In HONOR of

MAHIN ARYEH

Matriarch of the Family
In good health may she continue
maychial lechial, from strength to strength
as our source of pride and inspiration

DEDICATED TO OUR MOTHERS

ZARA MORADI GHADAMIAN
and
EDNA SHIRAZIAN

WHOSE LOVE AND DEVOTION
SUSTAIN US and WHOSE MIDOT CONTINUE TO INSPIRE US

EDWIN YOSEF and BIANCA FREIDA SHIRAZIAN

DEDICATED TO MY AISHES CHAYIL,

CINDY HODKIN

WITH LOVE,
MORRIS

DEDICATED TO ELEVATE THE NESHAMA OF

NISIM BEN ABRAHAM

by Dr Isaac Sachmechi

IN HONOR OF
THE SHINING LIGHT IN OUR LIFE,
OUR MOTHER AND MENTOR, פרח

FERRY SEDAGHATPOUR